Reflections of a Sister

and

Proof of the Afterlife

By

Pamela B Cherry

All rights reserved. This book or any portion thereof may not be reproduced or used in any manner whatsoever without the express written permission of the author except for the use of brief quotations in a book review.
Copyright © 2016 Pamela B Cherry

INTRODUCTION

I wrote this book to pass on the experiences that I have had. To show people that they might also experience similar but don't recognize them as anything out of the norm. I am a very ordinary person; I don't have any special gifts more than anyone else. I have learned, however, that these gifts are within each and every one of us. It is necessary to learn how to recognize what is happening around us and in our heads. We need to 'hear' and 'see' that which is not obvious to us as we rush through each day, carrying out our regular chores. We need to develop, cultivate and improve these gifts.

Everyone has a Guiding Spirit, from when they are born, but if asked, many will reply that they have never thought about this and are certainly not aware or in contact with such a being. This is similar to having a friend trailing around beside you all your life, a friend who is ready to help you as soon as you ask, a friend to talk to in times of trouble or confusion, a friend who will help you to see the solution to a problem – who expects no reward and demands nothing from you, yet this friend is totally ignored.

I used to be skeptical and continually searched for proof, well, in this book I have put together a sample of experiences that have proved to me beyond a doubt that there is only a gossamer veil between us and those who have passed over.

SISTERS

Sisters come in all kinds of packages and bearing that in mind I think that the relationship that I had with Audrey was fairly average, but at the same time, it wasn't. We were sisters; we shared family blood, an older sister, a wonderful mother and father. However, Audrey was just over twelve years older than me so we didn't share most things that sisters of similar age do. Of course, in our early childhood, even one or two years makes a huge difference.

I wasn't aware that I might have a different relationship with my sisters, than any of my friends. I was a happy kid with three mothers who were always there to look after me and spoil me.

It must have been somewhat annoying for both my sisters to have to mind this little kid when our mother went out, or away for a week with dad who was a commercial traveller. I was never aware of any animosity though and have wonderful memories of the great times I had with both my sisters.

I do have one amusing memory of Audrey being very annoyed with me. When I was about five or six, she used to walk me to school some mornings, on her way to college. One morning, a car stopped and the driver who was a friend of Audrey's asked if we would like a lift. Audrey was delighted and told me to get into the car, but I absolutely refused.

My parents had told me that I was never to get into the car of a stranger and I didn't know this person, so, with the determination of a five or six-year-old, I made it clear that there was no way I was getting into the car. They spent a few minutes trying to convince me that it was OK but I adamantly refused. I remember Audrey grumbling at me, as she continued to walk me to school, but she wasn't really too cross.

I got teased and tricked and bossed around but it was all lighthearted banter and my innocence probably gave them some amusement. There were also lots of treats, like the absolutely huge Easter egg I got when I was about four or five. The chocolate egg was half as big as I was. Sweets and books and clothes and toys, I was a very lucky little girl. Best times were at Christmas. The tree never got dressed until Christmas Eve. The big girls were dating by the time I was of an age to understand about surprises and Santa. It became the tradition for one or other of my sisters and their boyfriend to take me out of the house on Christmas Eve.

Usually they took me to a movie or a pantomime, afterwards, there would always be a visit to a 'Café', one of those real American type Cafés with all the bright pink, blue and yellow lights, where I would get Knickerbocker Glory in a glass nearly as big as I was. Ooooh, those were the days!

Then the sisters got married complete with little sister as bridesmaid, I was truly made up. Visits and holidays were followed closely by my adolescence, independence and spending more time with my own friends.

The years slipped by and I learned bit-by-bit that perhaps the bond I thought was so strong between me and Audrey was not quite as I thought. Both of my sisters lived through relatively hard times during the war, even though Ireland was neutral, there was a shortage of much that we now take for granted and rationing was in place.

Being the youngest I was very spoilt, and of course, I had a lot of opportunities that were never available to my sisters. Through my forties and fifties, Audrey and I had a lot of ups and downs, sad to say there were more downs than ups. Unfortunately, Audrey developed a type of depression, Mum recognised what was wrong with her and understood her sometimes-erratic behaviour, but I didn't. Audrey said to me a few weeks ago, through a medium, that she wished she had been more vocal about how she felt, as it would have made life much easier. In the late twentieth century, problems like depression were not spoken about. These days it is far more understood and those who suffer can get help through support groups and medication.

Audrey did leave her mark on this world, four wonderful daughters who have now raised their own kids, eleven in total. She competed at the top level in badminton then moved on and became a great golfer; she loved to ski, was an international bridge player and would test her memory by regularly reciting over 10 minutes of a poem that she would have learned. In addition to this, she was also an astute businesswoman.

Being a keen and excellent badminton player, Audrey spent a lot of time enjoying this sport. It was through badminton that she met her soul mate John Hopkins. John was very good to me, and at seven years old, I was convinced and told Audrey so, that I was going to grow up very quickly and marry John before she did. I really believed I could do this. Hard as I tried, I could not grow up any quicker and when I was nine Audrey and John got married, with me in tow as the bridesmaid of course.

The Hopkins family has carried out business in Wicklow town for nearly two hundred years, starting up a shop on the main street in the 1850s. John was now managing the shop and it was a very successful. Audrey quickly took an interest in the family retail business and tried some ideas of her own, commencing with selling a few dolls, games and children's toys at Christmas. She continued to build Hopkins Toymaster into a very successful and popular store over the following twenty, twenty-five years. The store was the main attraction for people who were looking to buy toys, books or crafts from within a hundred miles radius or more.

Every Christmas, I used to look forward to working in the shop, especially in the early years when Santa was a big attraction. Parents and kids would be lined up to visit Santa, down the stairs and out onto the street. Each year there would be a different theme and I would be the person sending the appropriate parcel through, or up to Santa, coloured tickets indicated what parcel would be appropriate.

Nights were spent wrapping up hundreds of parcels for the anticipated visitors. It was indeed, a sad day when Hopkins decided that Santa would not be visiting the store anymore. Unfortunately more shopping centres and big stores were popping up in Dublin, roads and infrastructure improved, shopping malls and centres opened and business for the 'down country' families reduced. Even so, Hopkins Toymaster is still very viable and the favourite place for most kids to visit.

So, Audrey and I had our ups and downs, she passed over very unexpectedly and suddenly in 2007. I am glad to say that over the few years before her passing, we were on better terms. She was the best of company when she was in good form, lots of laughs and great fun.

It was a terrible shock when Robert and I got the news and it is very sad to think that she was only 72 at the time, with so much more living to do. Anyway, that is how it is, when our time is up, we must go and prepare for the next chapter.

Recently, I learned that when one passes suddenly, it can be a shock for the soul that passes over, therefore it goes to a resting/recovery chamber for however long the recovery takes, could be days or could be years. I like to think this is what happened to Audrey.

FEATHERS

Commencing from March of 2008 on my birthday, I started finding little white feathers in places where no feather should or could have been. Audrey was always one who collected feathers if she found them when out walking or golfing etc.

This love of feathers started when she was a baby, only just walking. If she found a feather, she would pick it up and tickle her nose with it. She preferred the little white fluffy feathers. This became a habit, in that when going to sleep, she would always tickle her nose with the latest feather. I must add she ceased this exercise once she was beyond baby days. Because of this I never had any doubt that she was sending the feathers to me.

For all of my life I have never found feathers as I have since Audrey passed over. In the following pages, I have outlined some of the very strange places where little white feathers have turned up.

BIRTHDAY FEATHER – MARCH 2008

In 2008 Robert and I were living in a house in Brittany France. We were renovating and decorating. It was a cold March morning when I went out of our hall door to check the post box. It was my birthday. There on the mat was a little soft fluffy feather.

"Happy Birthday" from Audrey?

The mat in question was at the top of some enclosed steps and yes; the feather could have blown in from anywhere. The fact is though, that for the past eighteen months of living there, I had never seen a similar feather anywhere, never mind on the front doormat.

VIETNAM FEATHERS

We were shopping for some conservatory chairs and came across one wickerwork chair that was exactly what we were looking for. The shop assistant told us that this particular chair was made in Vietnam and only delivered to order. We ordered four and waited for the call to say that they had arrived.

Two weeks later we received word and Robert returned to the shop to pick up the four chairs. They were wrapped completely in soft clear plastic wrap. He intended collecting them in our spacious car, but it wasn't as easy as he had expected, as he had to maneuver them around to get them in.

He nearly fell over, when he turned one of the chairs on it's side and revealed, stuck in the under-side of the seat, a little white feather!

A chair came all the way from Vietnam, and a feather all the way from Heaven.

ROCK FEATHERS

We were out at the beach at Frehal, one summers day. There is a jetty that is about one hundred yards long, for people to put little boats out. The tide goes out about eighty yards, hence the reason for the long jetty. After walking the beach, we took an amble down the jetty to watch some families launching their little boats and some fishermen cleaning and gutting their catch. The exposed rocks alongside the jetty were very pretty, some with seaweed on and other of different colours. I got out my camera to take some photographs but decided to just pick out one rock that looked really special – otherwise, I would have loads of rock photos to choose from.

When I got home I downloaded the photographs onto my computer, and set about cropping and describing each one.

Well, "knock me down with a feather," as they say! When I cropped and enlarged the photo I had taken of the rocks, what do you think I could see, stuck on it? Guessed right! A little white feather! Invisible to my naked eye, but when enlarged, there it was. Of all the rocks I could have photographed, I got the one with the feather………. Or did the one with the feather get me?

SUPERMARKET FEATHERS

One summers day Robert and I decided to go to IKEA. We stopped at a supermarket to do some shopping before returning home. It wasn't our regular store; in fact, we had never shopped there before. We bought some very nice lemon flavoured organic biscuits, or 'cookies as they are called in the USA. We had not seen the biscuits in any other store and kept saying that we must go back and get some more.

Several weeks later, in need of some supplies, we decided to take a drive back to the same supermarket, get what we needed and to treat ourselves to a few more packets of the Lemon biscuits.

When we went in to the store I told Robert that I wanted to go buy some seeds in the garden section and I would meet him in the biscuit section. As I walked over to where I could see Robert standing, I wondered why he was just standing still, gazing at the display. He suddenly saw me approaching and started pointing wildly at the biscuits.

"What is it?" I said to him from about 30 feet away.

"You won't believe this!" He replied, still pointing dramatically at something on the display stand.

REFLECTIONS OF A SISTER & PROOF OF THE AFTERLIFE

When I was beside him I could see the organic biscuits nicely displayed in sections of different flavours and size of packet. The lemon flavoured ones that we were going to buy, were on a shelf about six feet from the ground - two shelves from the top. Sitting on the top of the packet of biscuits, the very packet that we would be selecting, because it was the Lemon flavour (!!!!) were three little white feathers!

We couldn't believe it; we both went weak at the knees I can tell you. Where did those feathers come from, as there are no birds in this supermarket? How come these feathers were sitting right on the very packet of biscuits that we were going to buy and how did the feathers manage to stay there so precariously balanced?

I took a photo to demonstrate, but unfortunately I couldn't show the biscuits on a shelf 'two shelves' lower as this supermarket didn't have such high shelving – but I am sure you can see how amazing it was that the feathers were on top of 'our' biscuits and with more shelves above!

THE BLACK FEATHER

I always get those little fluffy white feathers – BUT in 2013 Robert and I went to Ireland for a short break. Silly me got mixed up on the return date and we arrived at the Ferry in Rosslare, one day early. Not a problem as there is loads to see and do in Ireland, no matter where you are. All of the local hotels were totally booked up so we drove about looking for overnight accommodation. We eventually discovered a country mansion called 'Slaney Manor,' hidden away off the beaten track with lots of rooms available. What an idyllic place, with beautiful views and only peaceful country sounds to hear. The house has a lot of history with creaky floors and large rooms with high ceilings. We took long walks around the grounds and came on a building like a mini castle with battlements. This was the restoration of a twelfth century Norman Castle, particularly re-built to attract business for weddings. The owner of Slaney Manor asked if we would like to see inside and of course we accepted. He showed us over the big hall with the open fireplaces and upstairs where there were other reception rooms. We came back down the wooden staircase into another reception room with a double-sided open fireplace. As we were leaving the room, I noticed a black feather under one of the chairs that were set around the walls of the room. I pointed out the feather to Mr. Caulfield and asked if he knew how it might have got there, or was it a regular occurrence to find feathers inside like this? He made a face, shaking his head and admitted that he couldn't figure out how it got there as the doors had all been closed since the place had been cleaned last. I retrieved the long sleek black feather and we ambled back to the main house and to our room. When I checked my email a short time later, I was very sorry to read a message from my cousin, advising that her brother Bob, had passed away a couple of hours earlier. Audrey and Bob had been very close and always got on so well. During the war, he, his sister and another cousin were sent over to Dublin to stay with my parents, as happened many kids at that time. Audrey and Bob, although only aged around seven or eight at the time formed a lasting bond.

I believe this was another feather from my sister, black; to mark our cousin's passing.

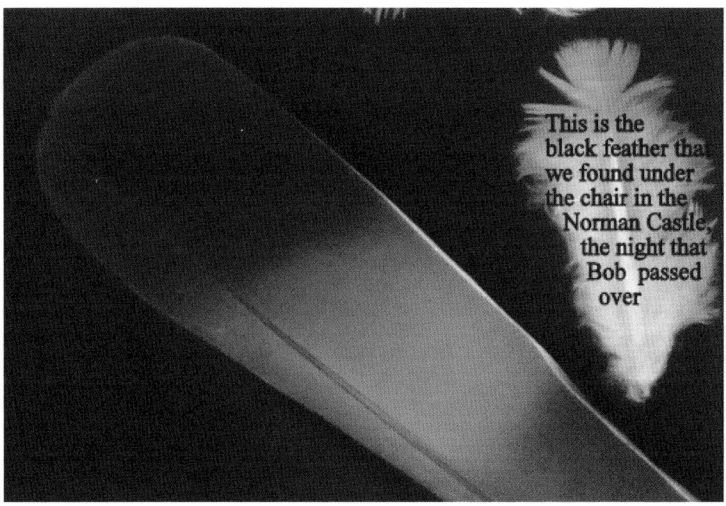

This is the black feather that we found under the chair in the Norman Castle, the night that Bob passed over

FEATHER ON A STICKY NOTE

We were in Florida in 2013. I opened the front door of our house to go out to the post box and there, on the doormat was a little white feather. I was just about to thank Audrey when I noticed that there were other feathers on the grass a few feet away. A little bird had met its end.

I said to Audrey, "I don't know if that feather is from you, but I'm afraid it doesn't count because there are other feathers too close. I can only recognise feathers from you when they are on their own and in a place where I wouldn't expect to find one."

The day carried on as normal, friends came over to visit in the afternoon. That evening Robert and I were going for a walk when I saw a piece of paper lying on the driveway. I went over and picked it up. It was one of those sticky pad notes.

On one side was written, 'Pamela Cherry' and underneath that was written 'Repossession.'

This could have been a note that fell out of our friend's car, they may have jotted down the name of my book on the note. That is my only explanation of where the note came from, however, on the backside of the note, stuck to the sticky bit…was…a … little white fluffy feather!

I roared laughing; it was as if Audrey was saying….

"Is this good enough for you? It even has your name on it!"

In relation to where the other feathers had been in the morning, this note was all the way around the other side of the house.

I have found feathers in all sorts of peculiar places. For instance, only the other day we opened up a carton of eggs that we bought in the supermarket. Although they may have been 'free-range' the eggs were packed in a factory, not by individuals at a farm. Stuck to one of these eggs was a beautiful little feather. So, I hear you say, what can be strange about finding a little hen's feather stuck to a hen's egg, in a box of hens' eggs? But let me ask you a question. How many times have you found a feather stuck to an egg in a box that you bought in a supermarket? I can't remember ever finding a feather under those circumstances.

Today, I opened the window; a feather flew by and then into the room.

The African Violet

My husband and I were shopping in Lidl's one day; I stopped to look at the plants. On a shelf on the other side of the display stand I saw a beautiful African Violet. Immediately I had two thoughts that it was very beautiful, but as we are away a lot, I don't like to buy houseplants. However, for some reason I went around to the other side of the stand and examined the plant more closely. Intertwined and hidden amongst the leaves was a little white feather! How could I 'not' buy it after that? It is still flourishing and has the most beautiful luminous blue flowers. I call it my 'Audrey' violet.

SMURLIGHT

I have always been interested in psychics, ever since my mother and I went to see a lady who lived in a block of tenement flats down the back end of Dublin. She was like an old gypsy with a very weather worn face, but there was nothing weather worn about her vision. She told us both things about our lives, past, present and future that amazed us as they were true or came true. But one has to be very selective about the psychic one visits, unless it is just for fun. I never go to those who advertise on the side of the road, I feel that if the psychic is really good, he or she will be so busy from word of mouth; there would be no need to advertise.

When I returned from living in Canada my niece told me about an Iranian lady who was very gifted, of course I made an appointment and I was so impressed, there followed about fifteen years of annual visits to find out what was coming up next. She was absolutely incredible, telling me about things that she would have absolutely no way of knowing other than through her gift. She introduced me to a medium that was also incredibly gifted, and enlightened me to the fact that I had many angels looking after me. I asked about my guiding spirit, who it was and if it had a name. She told me that he was a very old spirit and although they don't need names, he said I could call him 'Smurlight' if I needed to have a name.

Well, this started the first few steps into my spiritual voyage. I had heard people talking about us having angels and I did sort of believe it, but I hadn't really thought about it. You know what it is like when one is in their twenties and thirties and even forties, there is so much 'stuff' going on, not to mention working all hours to pay the bills. I was fascinated to know that I had this old guy 'Smurlight' hanging around me and helping when he could. I started talking to him, if I had a problem I would ask for guidance and the results were amazing. I might have been in a turmoil on how to solve a staffing problem or an argument amongst friends or staff, my mind tossing about from one solution to another: suddenly as if the mist was lifted, the solution would come to me. I very quickly built up a strong bond with Smurlight and realised that he is always there and ready to help, I just have to ask.

The biggest 'ask' was to please find a buyer for my house. In 2007 my husband Robert and I made the decision to leave Ireland and move to France. The financial crash was rumbling in Ireland and property was losing value. We had found a property to buy in Brittany, but everything depended on selling the house in Monks Glade. Robert and I were in Florida that May and June. Robert was very agitated as he could see the downward trend going on in Ireland. Regularly I would hear him say,

"We are never going to sell that house Pamela. We're

never going to move to France!"

I always felt a sense of calm when I assured him that we would sell, I had talked to Smurlight and he would make sure that we did. There was absolutely no doubt in my mind.

We returned to Ireland on a Sunday afternoon the sixth of July. Leaving the cases in the hall we went into the conservatory to relax after the journey and to have a cup of tea. As we sat chatting there came a ruckus at the hall door. Sounded like someone trying to get in. Robert dashed out and opened the door. Standing outside were three people, our real estate agent and another couple.

"Oh I am terribly sorry Mr. Cherry, I didn't realise that you were back," the agent said. "I was showing my clients some property nearby and decided to swing back this way to show them yours. I will make an appointment for them to come back later in the week."

Robert assured her that it was no problem, to just give us five minutes to tidy away our cases out of the hall and to clear away our tea things. We did this and made ourselves scarce while they looked around the house. The couple then went out and sat in their car with the agent for ten minutes before returning to the house and after a short conversation with Robert and me, we shook hands on the sale of our house. Now, I knew Smurlight would come through, but I didn't expect it all to happen within minutes of arriving back home!

Not only did the sale go through but also the process was carried out quicker than most house sales, despite existing peripheral problems with a license. Unbelievably, the sale was completed on the fifth of August and Robert and I were on a ferry out of Ireland, on our way to France, on the sixth of August - one month after meeting the buyer.

Everyone has a guiding spirit, from birth, this spirit is with him or her all the way through their lives, standing in the wings waiting to help and doing so without even being asked. But, as I said before, with busy lives, employment, families and all that makes up a person's everyday life, people don't have time to ponder on angels and guiding spirits. This is a shame, because they can make life so much easier.

Nowadays, it is easier for people to connect. There is so much support and information on the Internet and people are more informed. Even in my forties and fifties one was thought to be a little bit touched in the head, if heard to be talking about Angels and guiding spirits, not any more.

I would advise everyone to spend a little time to find out about his or her Angels and GS and to enrich their lives with as much knowledge as they can find.

THE NIGHT TJ PASSED OVER

Apart from feathers from my sister I have also had many other spiritual experiences. The one I had in Texas was the most startling and the most convincing for me, that there is definitely 'life' after death.

In 1995 my Mum and I returned to Texas for another holiday at the Mayan Ranch just outside the old western town of Bandera, which is about an hour north of San Antonio. We had been there several years earlier and had such an enjoyable time we decided to go back. The ranch is owned and run by the Hicks family. Don Hicks is second generation Irish. Don and Judy run the ranch with their 12 (then adult) children. Originally they had 11 children and adopted two local sisters whose parents had tragically died in an accident. The youngest of their children, TJ, had been injured in an auto accident at the age of 18 that resulted in his becoming quadriplegic, added to which he had multiple organ problems – lungs, liver etc. My story is about TJ who was about 25 when we arrived back to Mayan Ranch in 1995.

TJ used to get about in an electric wheelchair. He had his duties to perform, as his contribution to the running of the Ranch. Even though he had lost the use of his body below his neck, he was responsible to keep the accounts. This he did on a specially adapted computer, which he operated with his mouth. He had a companion who accompanied him, helped him do whatever he needed to do and slept in his room at night should he require help. He was mentally fully functional.

There was a huge family bond between all the sisters and brothers, of whom most were married and had children of their own. The family count was about 56 when we were there. The family ran the Ranch, and they did all day-to-day jobs. I never heard any harsh words or arguing, but they always greeted one another with hugs and smiles. Most guests only came for a two or three-day break, so Mum and I were quite unique in that we went for three weeks. We got to know the Hicks family very well and in many ways was welcomed into their family circle.

About half way thru our holiday a large group booked up the whole Ranch and they organised many festivities, sports and games. It was a real fun weekend. On the Friday and Saturday evening everyone retired to the Ranch Saloon. TJ was there and we got to know him a lot better. Up to this we had only exchanged minimal greetings as he was usually only about during the evening bar-b-q.

He was a good-looking fellow with the most wonderful head of wavy Irish red hair, which he wore to shoulder length. That weekend he joined in with a lot of the fun and we found him to have an exceptional sense of humour.

On the Saturday night in the Saloon we were chatting and exchanging jokes when TJ took off his cowboy hat and put it on my head,

'Wow' he said, 'That suits you, you look good – you can have that hat!'

Well, I was quite embarrassed as this drew much attention and I had always heard that a Texan never parts with his cowboy hat. Much as I would have loved that hat I replied that I couldn't possibly accept. After further insistence, and my continued refusal he put the hat on Mum's head and told her that she could have it, with the same result. Not long after this we were going back to our cabin when TJ asked if we would like to go to Mass with him the following day and that he would come and collect us in his special vehicle that carried him in his wheelchair! Well, Mum and I replied that we were not really religious and had not even attended our own church for quite a while. He then invited us to go to the local Rodeo in the afternoon with him but we said that we might go along but would do so in our own car, and see him there.

The next day dawned and Mum and I decided to do some sightseeing. We did go by the Rodeo but it looked very busy and we didn't think there was much chance of catching up with anyone we knew, so we decided to go elsewhere.

We went back to our cabin after the evening Bar-b-q and I

went to my room to bed, at about 23:00. I read for a while and turned out the light at 23:30 and went off to sleep right away.

Suddenly I woke up, the room was freezing cold! I couldn't understand it, as the temperature had been quite warm when I went to sleep. I quickly hopped out of bed to turn off the ceiling fan and to put an extra blanket on the bed. I looked at the clock and it was only 23:45! I was mystified. I looked outside to see what the weather was like. Sometimes if a sudden storm came in it would cause a cooling of the air – but nothing had changed outside! I got back into bed and cuddled up under the extra cover. Within a minute the room seemed to be warm again, stifling! I had to get out of bed immediately, put the fan on again and get rid of the extra blanket.

On Monday morning we went over to the main lodge for breakfast and immediately noticed that the Hicks family were terribly distressed, most with handkerchiefs at their faces and in tears. We were told that TJ had died the night before! We were so shocked! I was even more shocked to hear that he had died at about 11:45!!! Was this why I got the sudden 'coldness' in my room?

We commiserated with the family and told them that, as we were their only guests that day that they should not worry about us for meals etc. We would look after ourselves. They had more guests arriving in the evening and told us that the bar-b-q would be at the usual time. Mum and I pottered about for the day and at about 16:45 we went to enjoy some time by the pool.

Now, I must tell you that although I know how to swim, I am a natural born 'sinker'. Therefore, when I am in pool 'swimming' I have to concentrate fully on what my arms and legs are doing! While Mum sat on a lounger and read her newspaper, I was 'swimming' across the pool, with my head well out of the water and looking up – it was then that I saw TJ! The pool had several high Oak trees at one end and TJ appeared in front of the boughs about 30 feet from the ground. He was standing with his left hand in his pocket and his hat hanging down his back, his red hair was shining in the sunlight and looked absolutely gorgeous. Then I heard: -

"Tell my Mom I'm happy" Then again…

"Tell my Mom I'm happy." I was riveted – couldn't take my eyes off him – and then he just faded away!

I looked over at where Mum was sitting – she hadn't noticed anything. I usually shared everything with my Mum but this was so extraordinary and I guess I was somewhat in shock, so I didn't tell her. I suppose I also thought that she might think I just imagined it. To this day I really don't know why I didn't run over and immediately tell her. The other strange this was that the way I saw TJ was completely different to when one sees someone or something in their 'mind's eye'. He was three- dimensional and seemed physically very real. I suppose these days one could describe it as a hologram.

Anyway, we packed up and made our way back to the cabin to get ready for dinner. We headed for the Bar-B-Q. The family was huddled together in one area, hugging and comforting each other.

"Tell my Mom I'm happy" kept repeating over and over in my head.

Well, I looked at Judy and Don encircled by their sons and daughters. How could I go over and intrude on their grief by repeating my experience – I didn't know how they would respond.

We finished our meal and went back to the cabin. Mum was going to watch TV and I decided to go for a walk.

The whole time I was walking the voice pounded away in my head –

"Tell my Mom I'm happy." "Tell my Mom 'I'm happy."

Eventually, I said, "OK – I will make a deal with you – if I meet her I will tell her."

Within thirty seconds Judy and Don's 4-wheel vehicle came up a side road from the Bar-B-Q and turned back along the road that I had been walking. I should and could have beckoned to them and told them, but, didn't!

I continued the walk and the voice continued too. I was nearly back to the cabin and came to the place where there was a fork in the path. Straight ahead went to Judy and Don's house; the path to the right went to my cabin. I stopped. It was getting dark. The voice got more earnest.

"Tell my Mom, you have to go tell my Mom."

I felt as if I couldn't move, that I could not physically take a step on the right fork to my cabin. I stood there for a few moments and then said aloud,

"OK I'll make another bargain with you. I will go up to the house and if the lights are on I will tell Judy, but if they have all gone to bed I won't knock on the door!"

It was about 21:30 at this time. Now that I had decided to go to the main house I could walk again! When I got to the house it was clear to see that all the lights were on and when I walked to the main door I could see thru a side window that Don and Judy were sitting at a large family table with several of their adult kids.

I knocked at the door and when the door was opened by one of their daughters, I asked for Judy. Judy came out and I explained that I was going to tell her something that she could take on board or disregard, but that I had to tell her. She took my arm and we walked a little way from the house. She told me that she wanted to hear what I had to say.

When I related my experience to her she threw her arms around me and hugged me close. She said that this had made her day; she would now be able to sleep that night and rest in peace. Judy went on to tell me that the whole family had been praying all day for a sign from TJ that he was OK.

I returned to the cabin but still didn't say anything to Mum, why didn't I? Maybe I was still in a state of shock myself.

Next morning Judy came over to our table while Mum and I were eating breakfast. She gave me a big hug and told me that she was so appreciative that I had called to see her the previous evening. She said that the family was overjoyed when she passed on the message to them and that finally she had enjoyed a good night's sleep. They had concluded, that although the family had been praying for a 'sign' from TJ, none of them could have received one, because it might have been assumed that it was imagined and not real. Mum and I were the only people on the Ranch and therefore I was probably the most obvious one to get the message. I related the whole experience to Mum while we finished breakfast.

   I later learned that TJ's behaviour over the past few weeks had been most unusual. He had spent a lot more time with his nieces and nephews and took many of them on daily excursions in his specially adapted motor vehicle. Another peculiar thing was that although he was not at all religious he had started attending services and only the day before had sought out the parish priest (at the Rodeo) and went off with him for over an hour. It was as if TJ knew that his time on earth was coming to an end.

THE MOUSE AND THE GARDEN LIGHT

In May of 2001 I came home from work one day to find that a flowerbed lamp in the garden was on. Shining brightly out in the flowerbed. This light had never worked since two days after it had been set up several years earlier. I stood in my living room, frowning and blinking in surprise; I couldn't understand how on earth it was working.

My sister Gay was visiting with me at the time and I decided that before she had gone out in the afternoon, she must have plugged in the light and somehow it had come on. This didn't make any sense though. Why would she go into my sitting room and plug in plug, behind the settee, that she knew nothing about?

I pulled out the settee from the wall to check the plug. Ooh my goodness! Just underneath the settee near the socket was a dead mouse! I hurriedly pulled the settee further out and fetched a dustpan and brush.

Not only was there a dead mouse but also lots of what I later discovered to be about 50 'maggots'. Ugh! How disgusting, but obviously my cat had brought in the dead mouse or maybe a live one that had escaped and ran under the settee where the cat couldn't get it. Then it died! The mouse was but a shell of skin and fur as the maggots had done their job.

I had it all cleaned up and disposed of in a few moments. However, the thought of what could have happened if I had not discovered this little surprise. I might have come home from work one day to find the room buzzing and alive with

Bluebottles! That would have been horrendous.

When Gay arrived home I asked her how she had managed to get the garden light to work. She looked at me blankly.

"What light?" She asked

I explained that our uncle had kindly set up and wired in two lights in my flower bed, one of the lights never worked and we couldn't figure out why.

"When I got home from work today, somehow that light was shining bright."

I was beginning to 'see the light', to understand what must have happened.

Our dear mother hated mice, more than anything else. She wouldn't go anywhere there was likely to be a mouse. She lived only minutes away from me and it was not unusual for her to phone me to ask that I come over and remove a mouse that the cat had brought in. She hated mice so much that she would not even have a picture of one in the house, she would never keep a birthday or Christmas card that had a picture of a cutie little mouse on it.

Living in the country and by a golf course, her cat had a great time hunting and often brought her home a present of a live mouse. Snowy would bring it into the house and give it to her. Of course as soon as she saw him slope his way into her kitchen and saw his demeanor, she knew that he had a mouse in his mouth, I guess the tail was a bit of a giveaway too! (Smile) Mum would run into her sitting room and close the door, stuffing newspaper under the door to make sure that the mouse didn't escape from the kitchen. Next step was to phone me.

Sadly Mum had passed over a few months earlier. I believe that she was so disturbed by the mouse and the imminent birthing of the bluebottles; she simply had to get me to look under the settee.

The light, out in the flowerbed, never worked again after that night. I can think of no other explanation.

Can you?

Another memory comes to mind concerning my Mum. She was very fond of and close to her brother and was very upset when he passed away. A couple of years after she passed over, I had a chat with a medium. This lady told me amazing things about several of my ancestors including my grandmother, who left this earth over seventy years ago. The incredible news she gave me about my mother blew my mind.

"You know, your Mum is very happy, she is with her brother now and she loves him very much."

Then there was a pause for a moment...

"Her brother loves hanging out with your man. He loves pottering about with him especially when he's into the DIY."

This medium is a lady who not only lives in a different country to me, but also didn't and couldn't know anything about my mother or her brother or, for that matter, my husband.

I wondered to myself,

1. How did she know my mother had a brother?

2. How did she know the brother had passed on?

3. How did she know Mum loved her brother?

4. How did she know my 'man' is into DIY?

5. How did she know that my uncle was into DIY?

It still amazes me how anyone can do this.

A MONK IN THE HOUSE

In July 1989 I bought my little house in Wicklow, Ireland. A cute little dormer bungalow sitting on a rise in a cul-de-sac called 'Monks Glade'. A family who only used it as a holiday home had owned the house and they consented to an agreement whereby I could move into the house before the sale contracts were finalized. I agreed to them leaving what small amount of furniture they had in one of the rooms until convenient for them to remove.

One balmy night in August at eleven o'clock my Mum and I stood at the front door and waved goodbye to the previous owners as they drove away with the last of their furniture. It was at that moment that I smelled a most disgusting odor. I turned to my Mum in surprise and asked her what she thought that smell might be. We thought that it must have been coming from outside the house from nearby fields where farmers spread silage.

I took a few steps outside the front door and was surprised that there was absolutely no hint of the 'stink'. I returned to the front door where the odor was still noticeable. This time I walked into the hall and kitchen, but no odor in there. This horrible smell was literally within the area of the hall door. As quick as it came it disappeared and that was the end of it.

Over the following months the 'odor' was evident in

several different places in the house. I realised after a while, the odor only came when I was moving things about the house. I had many boxes stacked in the front room, every time I unpacked one, or when I changed the furniture around, there it was again, sometimes in the bedroom, on the stairs, in the kitchen.

The builder who built the house was a friend of mine, when I was visiting him and his wife one evening I asked him how the house was built and what was the foundation like. He confirmed to me that the house was sealed with a cement foundation. I thought that possibly the odor was popping up through air vents from the ground. Evidently not, I quizzed Jack as to what he thought it might be and when he had no solution I flippantly replied,

"Oh well, it must be a spirit then!" Jack looked at me curiously and asked, "Would you be bothered if it was?"

"No, not at all." I replied.

Jack smiled and then asked,

"Have you never wondered why that little cul-de-sac is called 'Monks Glade'?"

"Yes, I have, but I presumed it was due to the stories about the ghost of the Monk that is seen around the area." I said

"That's right. However, when we were building the houses in Monks Glade, I had a foreman who used to lock up all the houses and make sure that everything was secure every evening. One evening he came in with the keys, he was ashen faced and trembling. He told me that as he was closing up one of the houses, an apparition had appeared, in the shape of a monk. This man was very grounded, sensible and not given to imaginings."

So, that is why they called it Monks Glade. Several centuries earlier there had been a monastery a couple of hundred yards behind my house and evidently the Monks used to walk up to a 'holy well' situated only fifty yards to the front of the house. I guess the odor I was getting was the manifestation of one of these Monks.

My Mum said that the odor was because he must have had 'dirty habits'.

The odor continued to 'pop up' all over the house for several years. When it was there, I talked to it, but never got a reply. I asked if he wanted to pass over and offered the opportunity, but he preferred to stay. When I got a new carpet and a young man came to lay the carpet. During his break we sat and had a cup of tea and during our conversation I mentioned to him about the Monk spirit. I had to go shopping and left him to finish his work.

He was visibly relieved when I returned and had all of the windows wide open. He admitted that he has been scared and worried should the Monk visit while I was away, and just wanted to get the job done and leave the house. It never occurred to me that he would be bothered.

By the time I left the house nearly twenty years later the Monk had settled in and didn't get upset when I moved things about, gradually as the years went by the odor came less and less I wonder if it started again when the new people moved in after I left.

To you the reader.....

I hope you have enjoyed reading this little book and that the information herein, will give you some comfort should you have lost a loved one or do so in the future. Be happy in the fact that they are still with you even though not in a physical body.

We are all old souls who come into the physical body to learn and to gain experience on earth. When our lesson is learned and our time is served, we pass over into spirit, peace and love. So why should we as humans grieve, except for the loss of the human presence, especially if the loved one was trapped in a debilitating illness, enduring pain and discomfort. We should be glad that they are now released from the encumbrance of their earth body and able to fly free wherever they want.

Animals too go to spirit and can stay with us after their passing. I talked to a medium/psychic and she told me that my cat was walking beside me. I have had many pet cats and asked her which cat was there. She described to me perfectly, a cat that had passed over not long before.

I would love to hear from you as to your experiences and comment on this book. You are welcome to email me at o2bbizzy@gmail.com

REPOSSESSION

&

DÉJÀ VU

I have written two other novels that are non-fiction. The first one is called 'Repossession' and because I had so many ideas running around in my head, to expand the life story of the characters in Repossession, I just had to write a follow up book which is called 'Déja Vu.

Repossession and Déja Vu are both realistic, mystery, thrillers.

You will find them on Amazon, Kindle, Smash Words and several other on line reading systems. They are also available to order from all good book stores.

After reading please feel free to let me know if you enjoyed them, if you have any comments about the characters and would you like to find out what happened next?

Printed in Great Britain
by Amazon